A Biblical Approach to Life Planning

Dr. R. Henry Migliore
President, Managing for Success
Professor Emeritus NSU/UCT

Managing for Success
Tulsa, Oklahoma

A Biblical Approach to Life Planning
ISBN 978-0-9989006-0-5

Copyright © 2018 by R. Henry Migliore

Published by
Managing for Success
10839 S. Houston
Jenks, Oklahoma 74037
www.hmigliore.com

Printed in the United States of America.
All rights reserved under International Copyright Law.

On Course

The problem with life

is . . .

Life is a great journey

through places and times,

but some go through it

without a map or guide!

Life is a journey.

Let the Bible be your map.

Let God be your guide,

and you shall never stray from the path.

Roscoe William Migliore

TABLE OF CONTENTS

INTRODUCTION

The purpose of this book is to help people develop a long-term, biblically based strategic plan for their lives. My hope is to stir a vision or dream and then to provide a means by which that dream may be achieved. The theme is to prayerfully seek the Lord's will for our lives.

The vision for the book came after many years of work with corporations, businesses, organizations, and churches in which my primary focus was on helping them develop strategic plans and consequent methods to organize and manage. During forty years of consulting experience with these organizations—from top Fortune 500 companies to small businesses to church ministry, nonprofits, athletics, and higher education—I also had the opportunity to help meet the needs of people seeking direction in their own lives.

My previously published books outline the principles and examples from organizations with which I worked during that period. They are MBO: Blue Collar to Top Executive, An MBO Approach to Long-Range Planning, Strategic Long-Range Planning, The Use of Strategic Planning for Churches and Ministries, and Common Sense Management—A Biblical Perspective; and more recently Strategic Planning for the New Millennium. See my Web site www.hmigliore.com for other books and references.

As I counseled undergraduate and graduate students and people in careers up through top organization executives, I began to notice that I was, in effect, giving them the same advice I had given the organizations. I also noticed national statistics indicating that fewer than five percent of the people surveyed had any idea of where they wanted to be in five years. This prompted me to begin a research project of my own. Finally, this prompted thoughts on how to seek the Lord's call and direction for our lives.

Armed with this information, I began to see the great need that all people have to create visions for their lives, to analyze themselves, and to set up objectives that they want to reach. That is the major focus of this book: Where have I been? Where am I now? Where can I be if I systematically and prayerfully analyze how I can maximize my potential?

These principles will work at any stage of life. Grandma Moses painted her first picture at age 75, and Ray Crock was 54 when he opened his first McDonald's.

This book can be used to develop a plan for your life by following the outline. If further assistance is needed, DVDs can be obtained to guide you through the book. Audio tapes are also available.

The first section of this book is designed to allow you to gain a clear picture of yourself and to get an idea of how other people look at you. You will analyze people who have had an influence on you and what these influences were. As the book progresses, each step is like a small piece of a puzzle with each part not meaning a lot until it is fitted into the whole.

Thought and care should be taken at each step. The clearer the piece of the puzzle is, the better it will fit into the overall picture. You never know what little piece, such as a particular hobby or interest, might be the key to an expanded career or opportunity. Steps will be taken to determine things that make you feel good and things with which you struggle. Analyzing things we like to do and do not like to do further helps us have a vision of where we can be.

Then follow the same patterns and prepare an environmental analysis. This is the stage where you analyze what is going on in the world so that your plan can be based on good current information. A section is also provided for in-depth study of personal strengths and weaknesses.

You must analyze your strengths and utilize them. Your talents should not be wasted or misused. The planning process outlined and worksheets provided will help you make the most of your strengths and minimize or improve your weaknesses. By ranking goals, you can determine what is important to you on the job.

Based on the research to date, great improvement is needed in this area. This analysis helps you better clarify what you are looking for on the job. Because of the importance of occupation—careers or jobs—in people's lives, a major section is dedicated to helping you analyze your job and how much of your potential you are achieving on the job.

A very important section of this book is aimed at developing specific objectives and targets for the next five years in the following areas: career, family, health, financial, entertainment, and other areas of importance to you. This section is devoted to getting yourself on the ball and actually doing something.

This book is designed to force you to think about things you must do to get started: analyzing things that are holding you back, then working on a plan to overcome these obstacles. Another important section helps you identify people who can help with your personal growth. None of us can achieve our maximum potential unassisted.

Toward the close of this book, a very workable action-planning technique I have used for years is presented. This method shows how to take a target, develop strategies, and use a step-by-step method to get into action. It concludes with developing a way of rewarding yourself and your family as you accomplish your plan. I also recommend taking some of the personality and career tests available. One of the best is Communique,[1] which I have used in a number of businesses.

Remember as you fill out the book and answer the questions, there are no right or wrong answers, only facts about YOU. Also remember that each little piece of information is like a small piece of a puzzle. You cannot get a clear picture until all the pieces begin to fall into place.

Endnotes

FINDING SUCCESS IN THIS WORLD

Is success the mark of a Spirit-led Christian or merely the product of human effort? Does God expect our lives to be an overwhelming success story? Most Christians would agree that God did not create us to fail; after all He created us in His image. As such, we should have the mind-set of a success-oriented person.dd page header

Success at selfish goals is no success at all from a spiritual viewpoint. If we are seeking to please God—to fulfill scriptural commands regarding spiritual, moral, physical, financial, and other areas of life—then God expects our best efforts. Of all people on earth, Christians should be in the best position to rise above circumstances and to remain standing when everything around us has crumbled to the ground.

In his letter to the Christians in Rome, Paul outlines the troubles awaiting us in this life: tribulation, distress, persecution, famine, nakedness, peril, even martyrdom. Then he points out the distinguishing mark of the Christian: "Yet in all these things we are more than conquerors through Him who loved us" (Rom. 8:37, NKJV).

We are designated for success through trials and called to be "more than conquerors." However, this success does not come without effort on our part. In order to fulfill God's design for our lives, we must follow His outline for successful living, set goals in all areas of our lives, and be accountable for our plans.

A Good Plan

The prophet Jeremiah gave his fellow Israelites a hard message from the Lord: Prepare for 70 years of captivity in Babylon. Even in the light of the forthcoming hardship, God has a promise for success: "'For I know the plans I have for you,' declares the Lord, 'Plans to prosper you and not to harm you, plans to give you hope and a future'" (Jer. 29:11, NIV).

Just as God had a good plan for the Israelites, He has a plan to prosper us. How do we find that plan? God's word to Joshua gives us the key: "Do not let this Book of the Law depart from your mouth; meditate on it day and night, so that you may be careful to do everything written in it. Then you will be prosperous and successful" (Josh. 1:8, NIV).

Meditating on Scripture reveals to us God's outline for a successful life. "Success verses" abound once we start looking for them.

- ". . . I will bless you . . . and you will be a blessing . . ." (Gen. 12:2, NIV).
- "Commit to the Lord whatever you do, and your plans will succeed" (Prov. 16:3, NIV).
- "Humility and the fear of the Lord bring wealth and honor and life" (Prov. 22:4, NIV).
- "Seek first his kingdom and his righteousness, and all these things will be given to you as well" (Matt. 6:33, NIV).

In his book *Success, Motivation and the Scriptures* (Broadman, 1974), William Cook says, "Man was so designed that the only—way failure could gain entrance to his life was for him to consider some plan other than the plan of God and some other will than the will of God." Both Old and New Testaments offer insights to make a winner out of anyone. Our role is to find them, study them, and—most important—obey them.

Charting the Course

You may build the biggest, strongest, fastest, most luxurious yacht on the seas, but if you don't plot a course for it to take, the boat is just a hunk of wood and metal taking up space in the water. In the same way, our lives are aimless without goals to get us from one place to the next. As a management consultant to corporations and ministries, I have found that those who fail to plan, plan to fail. Goal setting does not guarantee successful results, but not setting goals will ensure failure.

Imagine an archer with an arrow on the string ready to shoot. The archer who aims at nothing is liable to hit anything, but usually not the right target, but an archer who carefully aims at the center of the target has a good chance of hitting the mark. Selecting a target and checking our aim is the difference between succeeding and failing.

God has a good plan for my life, and it is revealed throughout the pages of the Bible. Does that mean this plan will fall into place in my life without effort on my part? By no means. I want to be able to look back over my life and know that I did my best to accomplish all that God wanted from my time here on earth. The best way to be all I can be is to chart a course for success.

The first marker on the map of success is a vision or dream for your life. What is your heart's longing, your calling? Perhaps your desire is to be a teacher at the local college or to have your own business. Maybe your dream is to leave your well-paying job and go on the mission field. Your vision could be to raise your children in a godly manner or to pay off your debts. Without such a vision, the writer of Proverbs tells us, we will perish (see Prov. 29:18).

Do not be afraid to dream big, impossible dreams. Goal setting allows you to break a big dream into small steps. Remember, you can never do the impossible until you take the first possible step.

Next, you must analyze your environment. This involves simple research of the area of your vision. For example, find out if there is a market for your teaching skills or a need for you on the mission field of your desire.

At the same time, analyze your personal strengths and weaknesses—and be honest. Do you have a head for business? Do you have time and diligence to get that degree necessary before you can be a college professor? After this period of analysis, you can draw some basic conclusions. You may *realize* that there is a need for your business idea, but you cannot do it alone. You may have to change your dream to include a business partner. Or analysis may show you that you could best serve missions by staying where you are and providing supplies for those overseas.

Your basic conclusions now lead to goal setting. Some Christians think that setting goals removes God from one's life, but even Jesus set goals. "For the Son of Man has come to seek and to save that which was lost" (Luke 19:10, NKJV) and ". . . I have come that they may have life, and that they may have it more abundantly" (John 10:10, NKJV) are two of His stated goals.

Goals should be set in all areas of life—including spiritual, vocational, family, health, financial, and entertainment. Each of these areas can be broken down further. For instance, objectives for your career may include satisfying your boss, increasing your salary and job security, and gaining a promotion. Each goal should be specific, measurable, and deadline-oriented. Goals must be written down; otherwise, they are only dreams, not attainable objectives. Goals should be made for various time frames: today, this week, this month, or five years from now.

Examples of personal goals might be (1) to tithe 10 percent of your income; (2) to save a certain percent of your earnings; (3) to lose five pounds by the end of this month; and (4) to read the entire Bible in one year. Each of these goals is specific, and the result is clear. They are measurable. You know you have met your monthly goal if the scale reads five pounds lower at the end of the month. Goals are deadline-oriented. You only have 12 months to read through all 66 books of the Bible. To stay on the success track, you must constantly review your progress.

Consider a simple analogy: You want to drive from New York to New Orleans. So you get a map from the auto club, with every road you should take clearly marked, even scenic routes offered. You look over the entire map before leaving New York. Then you pack the map away in your suitcase until you reach your destination! How helpful would your map be if you never consulted it on the road? Would it not be better to review the map periodically to be sure you are staying on the right route to New Orleans? Of course! The same is true of reviewing your life goals.

Finally, you must work occasional rewards into your plans. Going from goal to goal without giving yourself a pat on the back leads to burnout. After reaching your goal of losing five pounds in a month, you may not want to reward myself with a hot-fudge sundae, but you might buy a new book or go to a movie. The promise of a reward for a job well-done can offer extra incentive to help you attain a difficult goal.

Being Accountable

Many people start down the path toward success with great eagerness and enthusiasm but lose ground because they are not accountable to anyone for their goals. We all like to think we are, but deceiving ourselves becomes easy when meeting a goal gets tough.

If your goal to lose five pounds in one month has not been written down and shared with at least one other person, it will probably be a hollow goal. How easy is it to tell yourself it is all right to eat that second helping of mashed potatoes or take that extra slice of pie. If you are accountable and if you report your weight weekly to a close friend who holds you to the plan, that pie will be tough to swallow. Accountability is not easy. It may involve sharing your most intimate secrets and confessing your most embarrassing failures. On the other hand, a good friend can be a great source of encouragement after a failure to lift you up and get you back on the road to success.

Meanwhile, do not expect to be successful overnight. Growth in Christ does not come all at once; it is a lifetime process. Organizations as well as individuals are healthier and sturdier if growth is gradual. I have known people who became overnight successes in their businesses simply by being in the right place at the right time. These people thought their abilities brought about success, but over time, their lack of planning, goal setting, and accountability wrote an unhappy ending to their seeming success stories. They did not discipline themselves for success in the long run.

Success in life is based on developing your strengths and applying them in service to the Lord. Goals are the map to take you to that destination. If you set your goals and follow them wisely and prayerfully, you will chart a path to success.

GOAL SETTING DOES NOT GUARANTEE SUCCESSFUL RESULTS, BUT NOT SETTING GOALS WILL ENSURE FAILURE.

Planning Your Life to Be a Winner
The Margin Is Jesus

"In everything you do, put God first, and he will direct you and crown your efforts with success" (Prov. 3:5-6, TLB).

1. God's Word tells us what makes the difference between success and failure in our lives. If you want favor with both God and man and a reputation for good judgment and common sense, then trust the Lord completely; do not ever trust yourself.
2. The difference between the winner of the PGA Golf Tournament and the 10th-place player is an average of one stroke; the 50th player only four strokes. You have to be a really good golfer to even be in the top 200, but a margin of only six strokes separates the top from the 200th player.
3. In a study of aerodynamics, one learns that the leading portion of the wing provides most of an airplane's lift. Of all the square foot of space in the plane, only this very small area up and down each wing provides the margin to lift the plane.
4. The launching of a spaceship is an intricate maneuver. Everything has to be exact in terms of the centrifugal force of the earth's movement, the launching speed, and the power as the spaceship is thrust into space. The slightest margin of error on the launch will cause the spaceship to be off hundreds of thousand of miles as it goes into orbit.
5. Everyone enjoys watching the summer Olympics. Many of the swimming events were won by a margin of less than a second.
6. If you study a football game, you will find that five or six key plays make the difference in the game. If the coaches knew which plays these would be, they would practice all week on those particular plays to be sure they were executed with perfection. The problem is that out of the 80 to 100

plays executed, one does not know which are the key ones. This forces players to precisely execute all of the plays so that the six or seven crucial ones are executed properly. The margin for winning boils down to a very few plays. For example, the LSU/Tennessee game was won on the last play of the game.

7. The difference between winning and losing in life can be measured by the margin. Whenever the margin play comes along, you will excel and, in the process, become all that you can be.

"IN EVERYTHING
YOU DO, PUT
GOD FIRST, AND
HE WILL DIRECT
YOU AND
CROWN YOUR
EFFORTS WITH
SUCCESS."

PROVERBS 3:5-6

THREADS THAT INFLUENCE OUR LIVES

As we journey through life, inevitably we cross the paths of those who have a positive influence on us. In my own life, there were teachers, coaches, relatives, friends in my church, and others who had a positive influence on me.

After a fishing trip to Mexico for the famed Lake Guerrero large-mouth bass, I began to see how the concept of the "thread of influence" and bass fishing share something in common. We are "hooked" early in life by positive-influence factors, and a thread follows us all the days of our lives tying us back to those influences.

In many ways, I was like the Guerrero bass on my first leave from basic military service in the summer of 1957. Like the big bass, I had wanted my freedom and joined the military service on my 17th birthday. I had come from a wonderful home with all the love and care that could possibly be lavished on a young, energetic, often unruly, sports-minded teenager. No matter how hard I tried to shake the hook, that thread of influence remained there.

When we were going into the city for our first leave in basic training, members of my squadron poured into a tattoo parlor, calling me names because I would not follow. As thin as that thread of influence was, I could not go in to be tattooed that day because of the thought of facing my parents. This is not to *say* there is anything so wrong about being tattooed, but it was not right for me at that moment. My parents had planted seeds of influence so that as I made decisions a thousand miles-from home, that influence of right and wrong was right there with me.

As I have progressed through life, many times the often thin, fragile thread of influence from another person's life has directed me through the temptations and trials that we all face as human beings. This concept of the thread of influence should encourage us all to hook as many people around us as we can with loving, positive contributions to their lives so that they will be inescapably tied to those influences as they live out their years.

I was further reminded how deep that hook gets set when I hooked into a big bass while fishing with my 18-year old grandson Channing. I could not help but look into my grandson's excited eyes, and think to myself, "This rainy fun-filled afternoon, I'm setting the hook even deeper in your life. Your granddad has a thread of influence you will never shake.

At this stage of our lives, each of our children and grandchildren are a real blessing to my wife and to me. For better or worse, they are energetic, independent, and excited about life. Like their father, they have an independent streak. But there is a thread tied to each of their lives and it will follow them all of their days. It can be a comforting, supporting influence.

The concept is obvious. Those positive, loving, guiding influences are there and you cannot get loose even if you try. All of us need to examine and acknowledge the threads tied to us by others, and be grateful. Then we should go about the business of tying good, positive threads.

MANY TIMES I HAVE FOUND THAT THE OFTEN THIN, FRAGILE THREAD OF INFLUENCE FROM ANOTHER PERSON'S LIFE HAS DIRECTED ME THROUGH THE TEMPTATIONS, TRIALS, AND TRIBULATIONS THAT WE FACE AS HUMAN BEINGS.

YOU ARE A GEM

Polishing the Gem Inside

The most precious gem was once buried in dirt. To be truly beautiful it had to be polished, cut, and set in the right light. In its original state, it was just as worthy, but its full potential was not known until someone recognized it and was willing and patient enough to set it free.

The right amount of polishing is needed to realize your potential. It is not necessarily what we see on the outside that makes anyone or anything a beauty; it is the glow from the inside. There is always work to be done, to keep on refining, polishing, and simplifying. Continue to emphasize those things you learn as you continue to refine and polish your life.

We owe it to ourselves to bring out the best of who we are—using our talents for something beautiful and worthy. That requires a staying power that comes only with vision and determination. For that, you need a plan. Here are the essential steps:

1. Have a vision or dream. You must have this so ingrained in your spirit that you believe the outcome is ordained.
2. To achieve your potential, get the facts and be aware of what is going on around you.
3. Analyze your strengths and weaknesses.
4. Set definite, measurable objectives.
5. Develop a list of strategies for each objective.
6. Put your plan into action.
7. Review your progress.
8. Reward yourself for accomplishment.

And you will find the jewel you are will emerge.

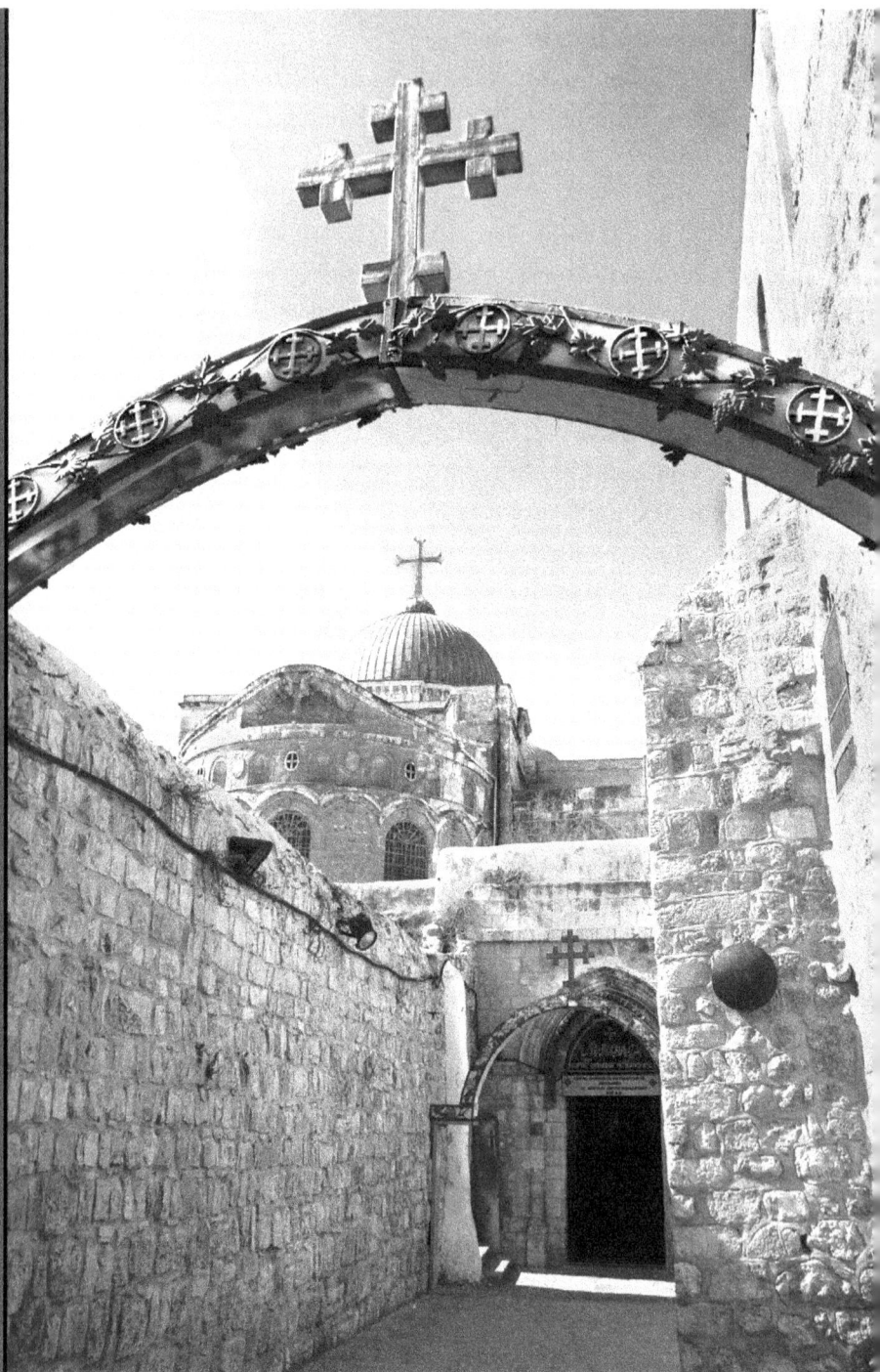

SPIRITUAL JOURNEY

Everyone who starts life goes on a journey. A spiritual journey is marked by people who affect our lives and are a great influence. I was blessed with a very positive supportive culture growing up in Collinsville, Oklahoma, in the 50s. Some like me have the opportunity to be part of a Christian home. Baptized at birth like others, I did not have a choice, but thanks to my parents I started a journey. Finally at age 11, at the First Methodist Church, I was confirmed. I can still remember that time today with vivid clarity. I could feel something in my spirit. I was given a Bible signed by the pastor. That Bible is still on my bed stand even today.

My mother Mary Gladys Migliore played the piano and organ for all church services. My sister Mary Helen Migliore became an accomplished musician and also played in church. My father Roscoe Channing Migliore volunteered and was on various church committees. I mowed the small church lawn as a young boy. At age 13 our pastor Cecil Bolding started working part-time at my parents' Western Auto store. This put me in daily contact with him as I worked there as a helper in a wide range of duties. It did give me a chance to learn from his wisdom. And we became friends for life. A few years ago we started seeing him on a regular basis, and he stayed in our home. That bond was always there. These influences continued to influence my spiritual journey.

In junior high I had a keen interest in athletics, and the Lord sent people my way. My mother wanted me to be a musician. At about 5 or 6 years of age, I took piano lessons. There was a failed attempt to teach me tap dancing. In seventh grade the decision was made to have me join the band and not play football. Everyone I grew up with was on the football team. This left me on the outside looking in, and it was a very painful experience. Improper behavior got me kicked out of band. I didn't have a bad start in basketball and baseball.

The summer going into the eighth grade, I mowed football

coach H. L. Goob Arnold's lawn as part of my summer lawn business. I liked him. His dear wife Lucy would invite me on the porch for lemonade. "Boy, why are you not playing football?" My response was, "My parents do not feel it is best for me." Mr. Arnold arranged a meeting in our home. He and Lucy were in church every Sunday and Sunday night and knew my parents well. Every week was Sunday School, church, and Wednesday night church again. My mother finally protested, "If he gets caught up in football and sports, he will quit going to church!" She was a mother looking out for her son. I still remember the next exchange. "If he misses church, he will not play in the game." I did get to play and loved it. From then on a ritual began. Even when I was a senior and living my life's dream playing four varsity sports, I still waved and said hello to Mr. Arnold and was reminded that I was in church.

The next step in my spiritual journey took me to religious services during basic training at Lockland Air Force Base in 1957. These services gave high school friend Mike Doyle and I an escape from the 22nd Squadron's rigorous training and discipline. In our family it was 100% attendance. It continued the spiritual journey for me to be there with my family and part of that wonderful church.

A major step in the journey came in 1970. My wife Mari and I left a promising career at Continental Can Company in Chicago to return to Oklahoma and teach at Oral Roberts University. Simple logic would tell you not to take a 50% cut in pay. I was comfortable and well trained in manufacturing and engineering and had no clue or training on how to teach in higher education. Coming into a ministry reinforced the power of prayer and how the Holy Spirit guides our lives.

Fast forward to our recent trip to Israel. We would see the culture and all the places we had heard about all our lives. As the week progressed I prayed in my spirit for a closer connection. The long flight was not too bad as we managed our way. From door to door, it was about 28 hours. Once there the action began. We were with a group from The Inspiration Network. This is a ministry founded by former students David and Barbara Cerullo. I am privileged to be on their Board of Directors. We have stayed close to them all these years. How do you narrow down the highlights after visiting all the holy sites? And what is the impact on us spiritually?

We had so many experiences in one action-packed week. We were on an old boat on the Sea of Galilee, and one's spirit could get a sense of peace gliding along the calm waters. It was easy to see Jesus and relive those moments. As the tour bus went from spot to spot in air-conditioned comfort, it hit me how hard travel was in those days. A walk from Jerusalem to Capernaum would take nine days. We gained first-hand knowledge of the history of the region and implications Israel has on the future of the world.

As wonderful as these experiences have been on my spiritual journal there have been hard knocks and unexpected turns. During a trip to Canada, I went golfing, rafting on the Kananaskis River, and bike riding in the Canadian Rockies. I had a simple medical procedure go wrong and ended up in the hospital with a sepsis infection of e coli bacteria. I was weak and very ill. Even in the midst of this uncertain time, my wife Mari and I covered scripture on difficulties, struggles, and problems in our Bible study:

We also rejoice in our sufferings, because we know that suffering produces perseverance; perseverance, character; and character, hope.

Romans 5:3-4

I consider that our present sufferings are not worth comparing with the glory that will be joy revealed in us.

Romans 8:18

That is why, for Christ's sake, I delight in weaknesses, in insults, in hardships, in persecutions, in difficulties. For when I am weak, then I am strong.

2 Corinthians 12:9-11

But even if you should suffer for what is right, you are blessed. "Do not fear what they fear; do not be frightened."

1 Peter 3:13-15

And the God of all grace, who called you to his eternal glory in Christ, after you have suffered a little while, will himself restore you and make you strong, firm and steadfast.

1 Peter 5:9-11

It was as if the Lord was giving me a hint, "Henry, don't get too comfortable with all the things around you." I am recovering slowly. I am weak but getting back my strength. Our pastor Tom Harrison preached on this topic and gave the same key points. The lesson for me: always rely on God. On my spiritual journey, I cannot bulldoze through obstacles but look to Him to for guidance.

Henry and Mari Migliore with former ORU students
David and Barbara Cerullo

Finally fall of 2010 and in Israel I realize the journey is not over. According to Bob Bufford's book *Half Time*, wife Mari and I are half way through the fourth quarter. Bufford describes life in the order of a football game. Mari and I want to live out the last quarter of the game as Bufford suggests "to play hard."

We will serve the Lord, be a blessing to others, and take our combined skills and resources and use them to serve the Kingdom. Bufford also says to spend time having fun. Yes, I am committed to what I like best—more fishing, hunting, going to athletic events, and travel. The scoreboard is running. Let's enjoy the game!

RETIREMENT INCOME

UNDER THE LAWS OF THE STATE OF
COLORADO.

✓ 401k
☐ Pensi...
✓ IR...

100 SHARES

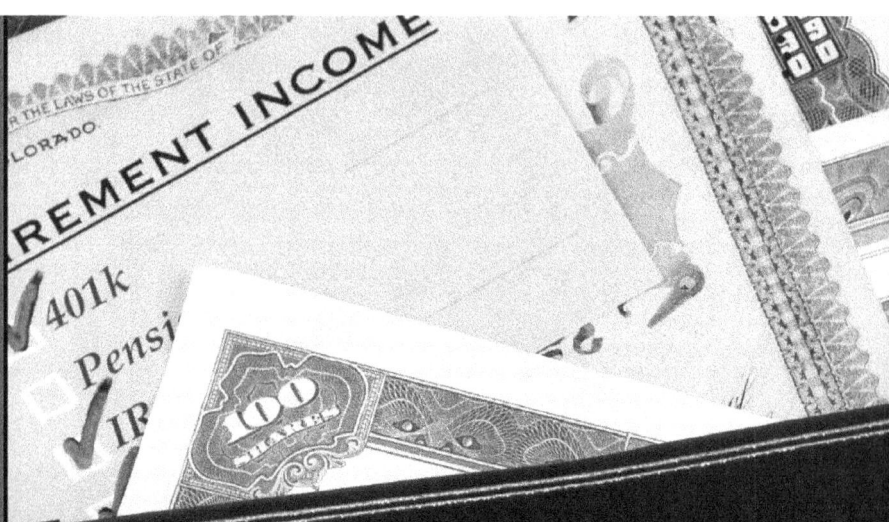

Financial Plan

Investments
Retirement Plan
College Plan
Insurance
Taxes
Estate Plan

THE PLAN—DEBT-FREE LIVING!

We all start budgeting with optimism and resolve to have a fresh start, do well, and succeed with the enthusiasm of a New Year's resolution. However, studies show that even when people make New Year's resolutions, they keep them for an average of only 42 days. Does this mean all of our visions, resolutions, aspirations, and dreams are doomed to failure? Only if they lack proper planning.

Making Plans that Succeed

If you really want to be out of debt, you can be assured God's Word is full of promises for your success.

- ". . . Seek first his kingdom and his righteousness, and all these things will be given to you as well" (Matt. 6:32, NIV).
- ". . . I will bless you . . . and you shall be a blessing" (Gen. 12:2, NKJV).
- "Commit your work to the Lord, then it will succeed" (Prov. 16:3, TLB).
- "Humility and the fear of the Lord bring wealth and honor and life" (Prov. 22:4, NIV).
- "The plans of the diligent lead to profit as surely as haste leads to poverty" (Proverbs 21:5, NIV)
- "Owe nothing to anyone except to love one another; for he who loves his neighbor has fulfilled the law" (I Corinthians 16:2)

What Is the First Step?

Without a vision of becoming debt free, you will probably never be debt free. You must see your goal. The first marker on the map of success is a vision or dream for your debt-free life.

Do not be afraid to dream big, impossible dreams. Goal setting allows you to break a big dream into small steps. Remember, you can never do the impossible unless you take the first possible step.

Next, analyze your finances. You cannot know where you are going if you do not know where you are. Once you know where you are, you will be able to set your goals.

How Do I Set Goals?

As with setting personal goals, financial goals should be specific, measurable, and deadline-oriented. For financial goals as well as personal goals, they must be written down— otherwise they are only dreams and not attainable objectives. Statistically, only five percent of people setting goals actually write them out. This may account for why so few people are reaching the goals they set.

Goals should also be written to include today, this week, this month, and five years from now. An example of goal setting for debt-free living might be: (1) take out my tithe when I receive my paycheck; (2) sow a seed to help someone else get out of debt; (3) put $50 extra toward paying down my VISA bill this month; and (4) pray prosperity scriptures over my checkbook every day.

Each of these goals is specific, with a clear activity and result in mind. They are measurable. Ten percent of your paycheck equals a certain amount of money. Goals are deadline-oriented. You know you have from morning until bedtime to pray prosperity scriptures over your checkbook. If you are trying to pay off your car debt, it helps to place a picture of your car on the refrigerator as a constant reminder of your goal.

How Do I Keep on Course?

To stay on track, you must continually review your progress. You can certainly expect some bumps in the road, but there is no reason to give up. You just keep going. Maybe you plan to be out of debt in four years, but it takes you five instead. So what? You will still be *out of debt!*

Will I Not Get Weary Along the Way?

Finally, you must treat yourself to an occasional reward. Going from goal to goal without giving yourself a pat on the back leads to burn out and abandoned plans. After packing your lunch and snacks for a week, you probably would not take the family out to an expensive restaurant to celebrate, but you might treat yourself to a sensible store-bought snack on Friday. It is an incentive to stay the course and keep on track. As part of the family budget, every member must have a part to play in accomplishing the overall goal. It not only makes them responsible and accountable, but it allows each person to celebrate the victory.

Being Accountable

As with many plans, we start with great eagerness then lose momentum. Accountability can keep us focused on our goals. For example, if the whole family has pledged to do certain things to save money, it is not as easy to stop by the local convenience store to sneak a snack before Friday. You are hindering the whole family from reaching a goal. Accountability can be a positive force. If you are accountable to others, you will also feel good about doing your part to help the family reach each goal.

One Step at a Time

Do not get discouraged if you do not achieve overnight success. When you run into problems, you will learn by overcoming them. When you experience failure, you will be stronger in knowing what to do the next time. Statistics reveal that lottery winners usually wind up in the same financial state as they were previously within five years of winning. It is not a matter of an easy way out. It is methodically changing your lifestyle that will guarantee financial victory.

Success in life is based on developing your strengths and applying them to the task. You can achieve your financial goals by mapping out a plan and setting goals to reach your destination. Through wisdom and prayer, you will be ready to make bigger plans and reach loftier goals when you become debt free!

LACK OF ACCOUNTABILITY IS ONE REASON PEOPLE START DOWN THE PATH TOWARD SUCCESS WITH GREAT EAGERNESS AND ENTHUSIASM AND THEN BEGIN TO LOSE GROUND.

Work: It Is Not All That Bad

Most of us, for a period of 40 years or more, spend about a third of our time working. By this, we usually mean working at some gainful occupation to earn a living or to contribute to family income. However, that time may be spent homemaking, although full-time homemakers are becoming fewer and fewer as wives swell the work force.

As Shakespeare observed, we all pass through different stages in our lives. In each stage, the work ethic takes on a different perspective to us.

The teenager usually takes a dim view of work. In an earlier day, the teenager's contribution was critical to the well-being of the rural American family. Large families were needed to survive in those rugged days. In today's more affluent society and with family work not available, young people generally do not contribute to the family's economic well being. However, if teenagers do not have responsibilities, they lose the opportunity to learn to be accountable.

Work has evolved into more of a process of learning, discipline, and pride. As a person moves into high school and college, work represents an opportunity to earn the means of acquiring what is perceived as indispensable needs: a first car, CDs, and extras that dad will not or cannot buy. When we set out on our careers, work becomes an extension of ourselves. Success on the job seems to relate to our success as a person. For some reason, one's worth to society seems based on one's job. At some point, after we have become somewhat accomplished as an electrician, tool and die maker, college professor, or electrical engineer, we become recognized for our craftsmanship and abilities. Here the work ethic takes on a whole new meaning. Work can become engrossing and something in which we take pride.

During these years, it is vital not to let work become so all-consuming that it distorts our perspective about other aspects of life. Too many people are successful in their careers but strike out as husbands, wives, fathers, or friends. We must work, but work should not become a devouring monster.

Finally, we phase out of the work force and enter retirement, the years we have looked forward to as harvest years, including leisure, travel, golf, and fishing, but all too often, disillusionment rears its ugly head. Instead of fulfillment, a sense of deprivation assails us when we are taken from our work. As retirement age gets lower and lower, more and more of us become susceptible to this problem.

If you hold the view that work is not necessary to your happiness, consider the plight of someone who suddenly becomes unemployed. It is a traumatic, insecure, and frightening time. If you are not sure how much you care about your job today, consider how you would feel if you would not have it tomorrow.

If we spend half of our waking hours at work, does it not make sense to put ourselves more wholeheartedly into it? If that much of our waking time is going into that particular activity, our efforts should be the very best we can put forth. Work should be taken as a natural, normal, and healthful function and as an opportunity to achieve.

One famous ballplayer said on nationwide television that he loved to play baseball and could not believe he was being paid to do it. Work might go better for us if we shared his attitude.

Scriptures on work:
- "But let every man prove his own work, and then shall he have rejoicing in himself alone, and not in another. For every man shall bear his own burdens" (Galatians 6:4-5, KJV).

- "…if any would not work, neither should he eat" (II Thessalonians 3:10, KJV).

- "One who is slack in his work is brother to one who destroys" (Proverbs 18:9, NIV).

- "He who tills this land will have plenty of food, but he who follows empty pursuits will have poverty in plenty" (Proverbs 28:19, NASB).

WORK SHOULD BE TAKEN AS A NATURAL, NORMAL, AND HEALTHFUL FUNCTION AND AS AN OPPORTUNITY TO ACHIEVE.

Twenty Sure Ways to Lose Money

After 50 years of helping people solve business and personal problems, I have discovered a few ways to lose one's hard-earned money. Listen carefully for these phrases, and your objective of losing money will soon be attained:

- This exciting opportunity is available for only a short time . . . .
- You have been selected as a winner of a fabulous prize. You must . . . .
- All your friends are in on this . . . .
- You have earned the right, through your success, to be considered for . . . .
- I am a (Christian, member of a lodge or club, and so forth). Do business with me . . . .

Keep talking to the person who uses one of these opening lines, and soon he or she will have—as a popular country song says—the gold mine and you will have the shaft.

Here are some rules to consider, if your aim is to lose your money quickly:

1. Let someone else, preferably someone you do not know, bring you the investment idea. If they come to your door, by all means, let them in.
2. Constantly worry and plot against paying taxes. Find ways to lose so that you can deduct the losses from your taxes.
3. Not promoting your skills, expertise and business.
4. Be arrogant and have a god-like air.
5. Try to get rich quickly.
6. For the ultimate experience, invest money you cannot afford to lose.
7. Respond quickly with action when your mate says, "Why don't you do as well as your brother?"
8. Give your mate and children credit cards and no budget.

9.   Send your children to college with no accountability. Provide a car, if possible. Keep them in college no matter what.
10.   Following up on meetings only using the phone and note using email, letters, postcards, and stamps.
11.   Buy raw land, the farther away from home, the better.
12.   Build your wife a bigger closet.
13.   Go into a business you know nothing about.
14.   Do not develop a personal plan, a financial plan, or set goals.
15.   Do not buy insurance of any kind.
16.   Do not make out your own personal will. Watch your loved ones from Heaven while they fight over your estate and give most of it to lawyers.
17.   Get a divorce.
18.   Do a lot of impulse buying.
19.   Keep all of your money for yourself. Do not give to your church or to any worthy cause.
20.   Do not ask for any advice from professionals in banking, insurance, law, investments, and accounting.

This topic is meant to make all of us think before we spend. We all have most likely made some poor economic decisions and learned good lessons. Our quality of life can be affected by our economic decisions. It is to be hoped that we will be more careful and think through how we invest and spend our money.

IF YOUR AIM IS TO LOSE YOUR MONEY QUICKLY, GIVE YOUR MATE AND CHILDREN CREDIT CARDS AND NO BUDGET.

Dinosaur Tale Told for Today

Consider the shifting rain forests in the ancient time of the dinosaurs. External factors changed conditions. Plant and animal life had to adapt. Those that stayed and survived as the land became more arid were the lizards, cacti, and other forms of life that could adapt. Some of the more mobile ones, such as birds and bears, migrated with the shifting rain forest.

The dinosaur, with its very small brain mass, did nothing. Dinosaurs could not assimilate information, see what was going on, and did not read much into the situation as they became uncomfortable in a drying up swamp. The lack of comfort did not trigger action. As a result, they became extinct.

Many of us, like the lizard, have adapted, survived, and even prospered during the shifting of the U.S. economic climate. Others, like the bear, read the handwriting on the wall, and have left for better job climates in places such as Arizona and Florida.

Others are caught in a seemingly self-imposed trap. Unlike the dinosaur, they are uncomfortable, cannot see what is happening but hope for a wide variety of reasons to be able to stay in the area. Hope turns to despair. Consider these things: What does the future hold?

What does this mean to us? State and local governments, chambers of commerce, and so forth, are going all out to improve education, attract industry, and help businesses succeed. Churches, ministries, and The United Way recognize the changing needs of people and work to meet these needs. City planners and school administrators plan for changing demographics.

If you are like a lizard and stayed put, and the nature of your business is adaptable, there is no reason you cannot prosper in the changing climate. As a matter of fact, these are times of great opportunity.

If you are in a dinosaur-type situation, you need to adapt or move. Adapting can take the form of luck. There are hundreds of responses to many local job ads. One person gets the job.

Adapting also can take the form of starting or working for a small business. Nationally, companies with up to 19 employees accounted for 82 percent of job expansions, and companies with more than 5,000 employees lost 13.54 percent net. As we enter this new decade, business conditions are not positive. Unemployment remains high. The rainforest could shift again.

A word of caution: A staggering 50 percent of all small businesses close within 4 years. Within 10 years, 85 percent have either failed or given up.

Small businesses overall have been successful. About 90 percent of the 16 million businesses in the United States are small, with annual sales of $300,000 or less. *Inc. Magazine* has identified 227 fast-growing companies in Oklahoma of 1,211 just started. It stands to reason that as these prosper, they will continue to need good people. It might be worth starting at a lower salary, proving yourself, and prospering as the company grows.

So develop a life plan. Determine what is important to you and your family. Recognize your career as a subset of your life plan. Make necessary tradeoffs and develop your plan of action. Things will fall in place.

DETERMINE WHAT IS IMPORTANT TO YOU AND YOUR FAMILY. MAKE NECESSARY TRADEOFFS AND DEVELOP YOUR PLAN OF ACTION. THINGS WILL FALL IN PLACE.

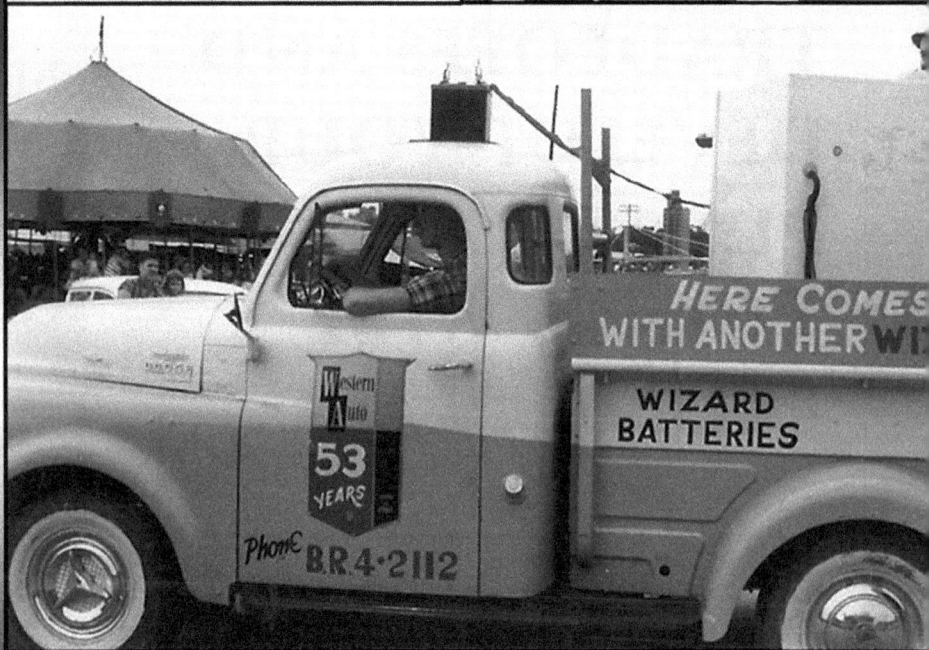

A COLLINSVILLE CHRISTMAS IN THE 50S

Growing up in Collinsville, OK during the early 50s was a treat. Old-timers will remember our father, Roscoe Migliore, who owned and operated the Western Auto store on Main Street. Our family worked in the store year round. Christmas week was always especially busy but exciting. There was a buzz in the air. Not many will remember because this was before Wal-Mart and the malls. Main Street Collinsville, Skiatook, Hominy, and all small towns in the area were the shopping hubs. Christmas week always brought out the crowds. For me it was fun because I would see friends and enjoyed the activity. As a treat we ate at Mrs. Bowman's cafe up the street. My jobs were putting things out in front, sweeping the aisles, and taking the deposits from previous day to the American Exchange Bank just up the street. This made me feel real important.

Christmas Eve I would take my week's salary, which was about $9.00, up the street to Bayouth's Department Store to buy Christmas gifts for family and friends. I usually got there just before closing at 9:00 p.m. My buddy, Tex Bayouth, would take my money, and all the staff started rounding up just the right gifts from my list. Since they were well acquainted with my family, they knew everyone's right colors and sizes. Gifts were beautifully wrapped with paper, bows, and cards. I would sign the cards and be on my way. It would take two or three trips for me to carry the gifts down and put them in the back of the truck. It wasn't until later in life that I realized they had to be losing money on the proposition. Our families were and remain very close today.

Many of our customers purchased toys on the lay-away plan. My job was to climb the narrow stairs that led to the attic and put those items on the second floor for easy pick-up. Christmas Eve was always a 14- to 15-hour day. One memorable Christmas Eve about 9:30 p.m., I noticed several packages that were not picked up. I shared with Dad my discovery. He remembered who they belonged to. We searched the phone book to find their number, but they were not listed. It was about 11:00 p.m. before we could close up for the night. Since Dad knew where the people lived, we put the forgotten gifts in the back of the truck and drove the short distance to their home. As we pulled in the driveway, the house was dark. I remember it was especially cold that night. We knocked on the door several times before the porch light came on and a man came to the door. He immediately recognized Dad. We told him we had his forgotten presents with us. As the man gazed at the boxes in our arms he said, "Roscoe we cannot pay for the gifts." Dad's response was simply, "Merry Christmas!" and we carried the gifts through the door and placed them inside the house. That old truck for that night was Santa's sleigh, our father was Santa, and I was the little elf. What a life lesson I learned that cold night in Collinsville. Be generous at Christmas! There are a lot of folks out there who need us to be their Santa.

THAT OLD TRUCK FOR THAT NIGHT WAS SANTA'S SLEIGH, OUR FATHER WAS SANTA, AND I WAS THE LITTLE ELF.

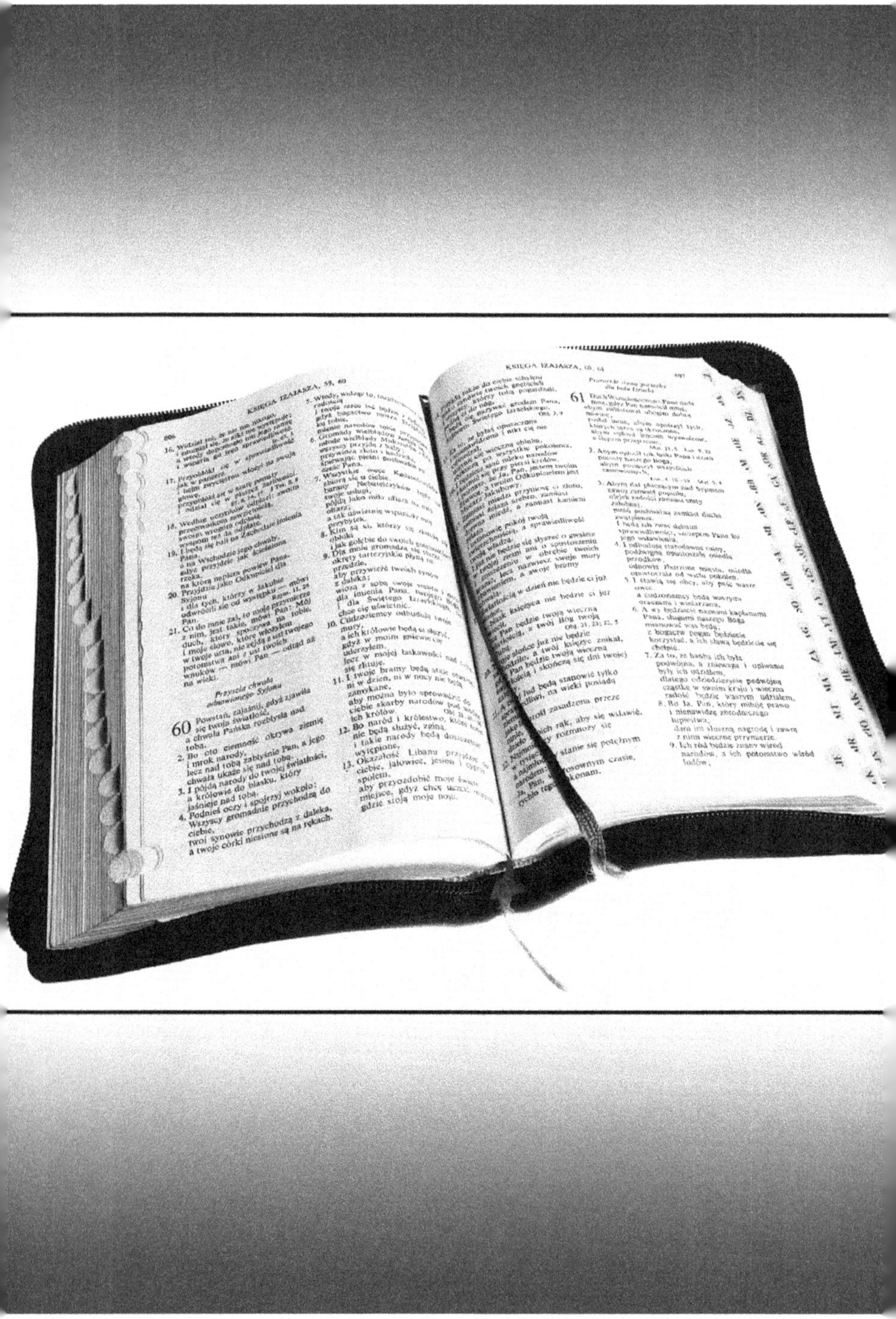

BIBLICAL OUTLINE OF PLANNING PROCESS

Purpose, Mission, and Vision

Proverbs 11:14:

> "For lack of guidance a nation [or a person] falls, but many advisers make victory sure" (NIV).

Proverbs 15:22:

> "Plans fail for lack of counsel, but with many advisers they succeed" (NIV).

Proverbs 20:18:

> "Every purpose is established by counsel . . . ."

Proverbs 16:20:

> "He that handleth a matter wisely shall find good . . . ."

Proverbs 29:18:

> "Where there is no vision, the people perish . . . ."

Proverbs 23:7:

> "For as he thinketh in his heart, so is he . . . ."

Joel 2:28:

> ". . . Your old men shall dream dreams, your young men shall see visions."

Acts 2:17:

> (Essentially the same as Joel 2:28.)

Romans 12:3:

> "For by the grace given me I say to every one of you: Do not think of yourself more highly than you ought, but rather think of yourself with sober judgment, in accordance with the measure of faith God has given you" (NIV).

Galatians 6:3-4:

> "If anyone thinks he is something when he is nothing, he deceives himself. Each one should test his own actions. Then he can take pride in himself, without comparing himself to somebody else." (NIV).

Ephesians 4:1:

> ". . . I urge you to live a life worthy of the calling you have received" (NIV).

Psalm 37:4:

> "Delight yourself in the Lord and he will give you the desires of your heart" (NIV).

Matthew 6:33:

> "But seek first his kingdom and his righteousness, and all these things will be given to you as well" (NIV).

Environmental Analysis

Proverbs 25:2:

> "It is the glory of God to conceal a thing: but the honour of kings is to search out a matter."

Strengths and Weaknesses

Luke 12:48:

> To whom much is given, much is required (paraphrased).

2 Timothy 3:17:

> ". . . Complete and proficient, well-fitted and thoroughly equipped for every good work" (AMP).

Objectives

Nehemiah 2:4:

> ". . . For what dost thou make request? . . ." (What do you want?)

Strategy

Matthew 5:15:

> Neither do people light a lamp and put it under a bowl. Instead they put it on its stand, and it gives light to everyone in the house (paraphrased).

Operational Plan

2 Timothy 2:15:

"Study to shew thyself approved unto God, a workman
that needeth not to be ashamed . . . ."

2 Timothy 3:17:

". . . Complete and proficient, well-fitted and
thoroughly equipped for every good work" (AMP).

Luke 14:28:

"For which one of you, intending to build a tower, does
not sit down first and count the cost? . . ."

James 1:23:

"For if any be a hearer of the word, and not a doer, he
is like unto a man beholding his natural face in a
glass."

1 Corinthians 14:40:

"Let all things be done decently and in order."

1 Corinthians 16:9:

"For a great door and effectual is opened unto me, and
there are many adversaries."

Philippians 4:13:

"I can do all things through Christ which strengtheneth
me."

Colossians 3:17:

"And whatsoever ye do in word or deed, do all in the
name of the Lord Jesus . . . ."

Proverbs 16:9:

"We should make plans counting on God to direct us"
(TLB).

Proverbs 16:3:

"Commit thy works unto the Lord . . . ."

Colossians 3:23:

"Whatever you do, work at it with all your heart, as working
for the Lord, not for men . . ." (NIV).

Nehemiah 2:4:
>". . . For what dost thou make request? So I prayed to the God of heaven."

Plan in General

Proverbs 15:22:
>"Plans fail for lack of counsel, but with many advisers they succeed" (NIV).

Proverbs 16:10:
>"A divine sentence is in the lips of the king: his mouth transgresseth not in judgment."

Proverbs 19:20:
>"Hear counsel and receive instruction, that thou mayest be wise . . . ."

Proverbs 20:5:
>A plan in the heart of a man is like deep water (paraphrased).

Proverbs 24:3:
>"Through wisdom is an house builded; and by understanding it is established."

Reward

1 Corinthians 3:8:
>"Now he who plants and he who waters are one, and each will receive his own reward according to his own labor" (NKJV).

Proverbs 13:21:
>The righteous will be rewarded with prosperity (paraphrased).

Philippians 3:14:
>"I press toward the mark for the prize of the high calling of God in Christ Jesus."

"FOR LACK OF GUIDANCE A NATION [OR A PERSON] FALLS, BUT MANY ADVISERS MAKE VICTORY SURE."

PROVERBS 11:14

The Red Sea Rules

Rule 1
Realize that God means for you to be where you are.

Rule 2
Be more concerned for God's glory than for your relief.

Rule 3
Acknowledge your enemy, but keep your eyes on the Lord.

Rule 4
Pray!

Rule 5
Stay calm and confident, and give God time to work.

Rule 6
When unsure, just take the next logical step by faith.

Rule 7
Envision God's enveloping presence.

Rule 8
Trust God to deliver in His own unique way.

Rule 9
View your current crisis as a faith builder for the future.

Rule 10
Don't forget to praise Him.

Morgan, Robert. *The Red Sea Rules*. Nashville, TN: Thomas Nelson, 2001
.

WORKBOOK

VISIONS AND DREAMS

YOUR VISION/DREAM

Describe the vision and dream you have for your life:

What we think about every day is a hint about our state of mind. Our dreams should picture what our lives will be like in years to come. A dream if strong enough gives us the determination to make it happen at all costs. It helps us stay the course. Also, when temptation comes our way if the dream is strong enough, we will think twice about yielding to temptation.

- "For as he thinketh in his heart, so is he . . ." (Prov. 23:7).

- "If anyone thinks he is something when he is **nothing,** he deceives himself. Each one should test his own actions. Then he can take pride in himself, **without comparing himself** to somebody else" (Gal. 6:3-4, NIV).

How would you describe yourself to someone you have never seen?

Would your friends describe you the same way? What would they say?

- "For **by** the grace **given** me I say to every one of **you: Do** not think of **yourself** more highly than **you** ought, but rather think of yourself with sober judgment, in accordance with the measure of faith God has given you" (Rom. 12:3, NIV).

List the three people who have had the greatest influence on **your** life:

1) _____

2) _____

3) _____

What was the major influence from each?

1) _____

2) _____

3) _____

List your favorite social activities and hobbies:

1) _____

2) _____

3) _____

List three things that have made you feel good this month:

1) _____

2) _____

3) _____

Write out a one-paragraph description of the purpose of your life. This statement is an extension of your dreams. For the Christian it should start with how you serve the Lord. It covers family relationships, career, and occupation. It should include health, ethics, and integrity.

- "But seek first his kingdom and his righteousness, and all these things will be given to you as well" (Matt. 6:33, NIV).

- "Delight yourself in the Lord and he will give you the desires of your heart" (Ps. 37:4, NIV).

- ". . . I urge you to live a life worthy of the calling you have received" (Eph. 4:1, NIV).

- "Every purpose is established by counsel . . ." (Prov. 20:18).

- "Neither do people light a lamp and put it under a bowl. Instead they put it on its stand, and it gives light to everyone in the house" (Matt. 5:15, NIV).

• **3 THINGS YOU LIKE TO DO:**

• **3 THINGS YOU DON'T LIKE TO DO:**

Describe yourself:

List three things you like to do:

1) _____

2) _____

3) _____

List three things you do not like to do:

1) _____

2) _____

3) _____

WHAT'S GOING ON ?

- WHAT ARE YOUR STRENGTHS ?
- WHAT ARE YOUR WEAKNESSES ?

Environmental Analysis, Strengths, and Weaknesses

What is going on in the world around you?

1) _____

2) _____

3) _____

- "Commit to the Lord whatever you do, and your plans will succeed" (Prov. 16:3, NIV).

What are your major strengths?

1) _____

2) _____

3) _____

- "For unto whomsoever much is given, of him shall be much required . . . " (Luke 12:48).

- "Complete and proficient, well-fitted and thoroughly equipped for every good work" (2 Tim. 3:17, AMP).

What are your major weaknesses?

1) _____

2) _____

3) _____

- "Pride goes before destruction, a haughty spirit before a fall" (Prov. 16:18, NIV).

List some failures you have experienced in your life:

1) _____

2) _____

3) _____

What do you see in these experiences that was less than successful?

1) _____

2) _____

3) _____

Are these failures holding you back?

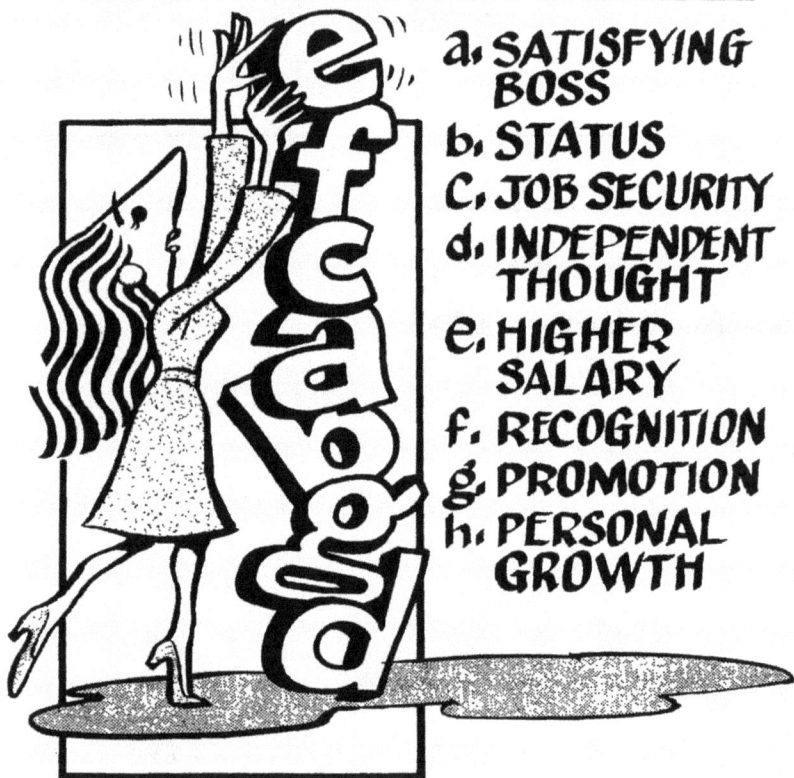

Your Work

Rank your job goals from 1 to 8:

_____ Satisfying my boss' expectations

_____ Prestige and status

_____ Job security

_____ Opportunity for independent thought and action

_____ Higher salary, more benefits, or both

_____ Recognition for good performance

_____ Promotion to a better job

_____ Personal growth and development

What do you like most about your job?

1) _____ _

2) _____

3) _____

How much of your potential do you feel you are achieving?

The Future

Write a one-paragraph description of how you want your life to be in five years:

- "A man's heart deviseth his way: but the Lord directeth his steps" (Prov. 16:9).

Write a one-paragraph description of how you want your life to be in one year.

OBJECTIVES:

(A) SPIRITUALLY

(B) CAREER/POSITION

(C) FAMILY

(D) HEALTH — WEIGHT, EXERCISE

(E) FINANCIAL —
   INCOME, NET WORTH

(F) ENTERTAINMENT —
   FUN, HOBBIES, VACATION

(G) OTHERS

HOW WILL YOU GET THERE?

Objectives/Key Results

In this section be specific. These are measurable objectives/goals/targets based on the foundation developed in each previous step from your vision up to this section. Where do you want to be . . .

A.   Spiritually:
        In five years

        Next year

B.   Career/Position:
        In five years

        Next year

C.   Family:
        In five years

        Next year

D. Health/Weight/Exercise:
In five years

Next year

E. Financial/Income/Net Worth:
In five years

Next year

F. Entertainment/Fun/Hobbies/Vacation:
In five years

Next year

G. Other:
In five years

Next year

Put Your Plan In To Action

- "Commit thy works unto the Lord . . ." (Prov. 16:3).

A.   How will you get there?

B.   What are four things you must do in the next few months to get where you want to be next year and in five years?

   1) _____

   2) _____

   3) _____

   4) _____

C.   What are four things holding you back?

   1) _____

   2) _____

   3) _____

   4) _____

D.   How do you overcome each of those four obstacles?

- "He that handleth a matter wisely shall find good . . ." (Prov. 16:20).

E.   Whose help do you need to achieve your potential and get where you want to be in five years?

   1) _____

   2) _____

   3) _____

- "Plans fail for lack of counsel, but with many advisers they succeed" (Prov. 15:22, NIV).
- "For lack of guidance a nation [or a person] falls, but many advisers make victory sure" (Prov. 11:14, NIV).

WORKSHEET:
- OBJECTIVE
- STRATEGY
- ACTION PLAN

Put Your Plan Into Action*

Use this worksheet to turn an objective into action.

OBJECTIVE:
(Make it specific, measurable, and within a timeframe.)

STRATEGY:

(What are steps needed? When will you start? What will you do? Break objective down into small pieces for an action plan.)

ACTION PLAN:_____

- "Study to shew thyself approved unto God, a workman that needeth not to be ashamed . . ." (2 Tim. 2:15).

- "And whatsoever ye do in word or deed, do all in the name of the Lord Jesus . . ." (Col. 3:17).

*Note: I suggest copying this page and making one worksheet for each objective: spiritual, career, family, health, financial, entertainment, and any other areas you desire. Fill out each sheet, and keep them in a prominent place. Some people have taped these sheets on their refrigerator or a mirror. The key is to keep them in front of you as reminders.

- WHO CAN YOU TALK WITH ?
- CAN THEY HELP YOU MONITOR ?
- REWARD YOUR-SELF

Review and Reward

I.   Review:

A.   Name the person or persons with whom you can discuss your plan.

B.   What will happen when you discuss your plan?

C.   Can he or she help you monitor progress?

       Yes_____ No_____

If yes, how?

II. Reward yourself for accomplishment! List something specific as a reward for accomplishment of some or all key objectives. Think of something that would be fun and give you a sense of accomplishment.

- "Now he that planteth and he that watereth are one: and every man shall receive his own reward according to his own labour" (1 Cor. 3:8).

- "For if I do this thing willingly, I have a reward . . ." (1 Cor. 9:17).

- ". . . Prosperity is the reward of the righteous" (Prov. 13:21, NIV).

- "So then, each of us will give an account of himself to God" (Rom. 14:12, NIV).

- "When the righteous prosper, the city rejoices . . ." (Prov. 11:10, NIV).

Conclusion

Congratulations! Now you have completed a long-range strategic plan for your life. You are now in a select nationwide group of only five percent. This plan sets you apart from the crowd. Now it is time to commit this plan to intensive prayer. The Holy Spirit will give you guidance on whether or not this plan and this direction are the ones that the Lord intends for you. You will find confirmation as you proceed through the plan.

Do not think this is a completed statement. You will continually revise your plan as you move through different stages in your life. A young person starting his or her career is going to have different objectives from those of a person nearing retirement. What you have learned are the strategic planning tools and techniques. You have learned how to seek the Lord's guidance. What you will do is continually upgrade this plan as you advance through life. Carefully study the biblical passages cited so you can better understand your life and be encouraged that there *is* a greater call for your life. Finally, this plan can give you direction. You have taken each part of your life and fitted the pieces together. Each step in the analysis, like a piece of a puzzle, does not make sense when looking at it separately.

For example, you might ask yourself, Why analyze my weaknesses? The answer is that when pieced together with all the other steps, the piece listing your weaknesses gives you a full, complete picture of your life. Every piece of the puzzle is important as is every step in this personal planning outline. Once you see where you are going, you then must pursue your dreams with all the vigor and heart you can muster.

Colossians 3:23 says, "Whatever you do, work at it with all your heart, as working for the Lord, not for men . . ." (NIV).

APPENDIX A

OTHER BOOKS AND ARTICLES ON CAREERS

The justification for organizations doing career/life planning with their employees comes from the theories of psychology. The basic hypothesis is that a happy, healthy worker is a more productive one. This is pointed out in the study done on auto workers in Detroit by Arthur Kornhauser and Otto M. Reid. What the employees need, in the eyes of Kornhauser and Reid, is "a purposeful spirit of trying to live up to their own personalities, to guide their activities in terms of future-oriented self-conceptions."[1] In other words, the employees need help with planning their careers and lives.

In Richard Bolles' book *What Color Is Your Parachute?*,[2] he talks about the job hunt, where to get help, where to hunt, and how to help a person begin to map his or her life strengths and weaknesses so that he or she can begin to find the career in which he or she will be happiest. The book is written in a chatty yet informational way, and the helpful material in the back of the book is often used by the CETA program to help young people begin to get their lives as well as their resumes together.

Self-Assessment and Career Development[3] by John P. Kotter, Victor A. Faux, and Charles C. McArthur emphasizes self-assessment. One form of assessment presented is open-ended questions: situations for reaction, reflection on past decisions, or active thinking about the person's decision-making process.

Another exercise used is 24-hour diaries, and the authors recommend highly the use of the Strong-Campbell Interest Inventory.[4] These are combined with text on the tests and what they hope to accomplish, as well as with sources of information for job searching to help people find and land jobs that they like.

In *Career Satisfaction and Success,*[5] the author, Bernard Huldane, outlines a system to help a person find his or her strengths and to use them. The system, called "System to Identify Motivated Skills" (SIMS), looks for the strengths "that are used repeatedly in experiences that turned you on." [6] Throughout the book, Haldane emphasizes the knowledge of these strengths to maximize one's career growth potential as well as one's own personal satisfaction with the job.

George Morrisey, in his book, *Getting Your Act Together,*[7] concentrates on setting realistic short-term goals and making practical action plans out of them. An important contribution is his concept of setting goals in bite-sized segments. Any discussion of this topic would be incomplete without the contributions of Ruth and Norman Vincent Peale. Dr. Peale's best-seller, *The Power of Positive Thinking,*[8] which was published 34 years ago, made a significant contribution to the idea that positive attitudes and a good self-image are keys to success.

The booklet, *In Times of Success,*[9] devotes one page to each of the following topics: Be Grateful, Be Loyal, Be Humble, Keep Faithful to God, Keep Up Standards of Honesty, Keep Working Hard, Keep Giving, Be Sensitive to the Needs of Others, Keep Things in Perspective, Sort Out Your Aims, Keep in Touch with Reality, Keep Remembering the Past, Keep Remembering All That Money Cannot Buy, and If It All Went—What Then?

In the article "Career Planning: Five Fatal Assumptions,"[10] Buck Blessing covers assumptions that people make about their careers. Also, Francis P. Martin, in *Hung by the Tongue,*[11] gives lots of career-related advice.

Roger Fritz, in his book, *You're in Charge: A Guide for Business and Personal Success,*[12] provides in a very thorough way, step-by-step lists and tips on how to know yourself. His chapter on how stress affects you and your plan is helpful. A few of his tips on stress are to tell the problem to a confidant, then relax—and only then do something about the problem.

Don Osgood devotes an entire book, *Pressure Points,*[13] to dealing with stress.

Dale Brown, a respected coach at LSU, has published five motivational books and has tapes and films available. Any of Coach Brown's material will help you go into action. I also recommend *Spiritual Fitness in Business.*[14]

Endnotes

[1]Kornhauser, Arthur, and Otto M. Reid. *Mental Health of the Industrial Worker* (New York: John Wiley & Sons, 1965), p. 269.

[2]Bolles, Richard. *What Color Is your Parachute?* (Berkeley, CA: Ten Speed Press, 1972).

[3]Koller, John P., Victor A. Faux, and Charles McArthur. *Self-Assessment and Career Development* (Edgewood Cliffs, NJ: Prentice Hall, 1978.)

[4]Ibid., p. 295.

[5]Huldane, Bernard. *Career Satisfaction and Success* (New York: AMACOM, 1974).

[6]Ibid., p. 3.

[7]Morrisey, George. *Getting Your Act Together* (Santa Monica, CA: Salenger Educational Media, 1980).

[8]Peale, Norman Vincent. *The Power of Positive Thinking* (New York: Fawcett Crest, 1952).

[9]*In Times of Success* (Grand Rapids, MI: Zondervan, 1979).

[10]Blessing, Buck. "Career Planning: Five Fatal Assumptions." *Training and Development Journal* (September 1986), pp. 49-51.

[11]Martin, Francis. *Hung by the Tongue* (Lafayette, LA: FPM Publications, 1976).

[12]Fritz, Roger. *You're in Charge: A Guide for Business and Personal Success* (Glenview: Scott, Foresman, 1986).

[13]Osgood, Don. *Pressure Points: How to Deal With Stress* (Chappaquah: Christian Herald Books, 1980).

[14]Brown, Dale. *Spiritual Fitness in Business.*

Appendix B

Comments From Others

"I'm excited! Although the seminar on Saturday hurt in some ways, it always hurts to have to change, and it was really needed in my life. Thanks for the opportunity to attend."

"This is just a short note to say thanks for your Personal Planning Seminar that I attended. The concepts you shared in the seminar were not new to me, but I finally heard them presented in a way that I could understand and apply. I am extremely thankful for the opportunity to attend a seminar like this and would highly recommend it to anyone wishing to make progress in their personal life. Thanks again!"

"I attended your seminar last weekend, and I believe it is changing my life. Saturday evening, my wife and I sat down and started the preliminary strategic plan, and it really set her free also. She had never realized the deep-seated resentment she harbored toward my handling of the finances."

"The material presented is practically applicable to life and covers significant issues."

"It really made me realize how important money is and the wisdom that is required in dealing with it."

"It makes you think about your future! How to plan for your future."

"It deals with the practical things of life that are usually not covered in other courses. Good, practical, real life information!"

"I enjoyed every single class. It was all very interesting things that I plan on using in the future."

"The course is very practical and very interesting. I was motivated to think about my life."

"The knowledge received was on practical life information."

"It helped me to realize the importance of goal setting, of being organized, and of planning for the future."

Appendix C
Personal Budget

DATE	JAN.	FEB.	MAR	APR.	MAY	JUN.	JUL.	AUG.	SEP.	OCT.	NOV.	DEC.
Housing												
Food												
Entertainment												
Utilities												
Phone												
Clothing												
Cleaners												
Haircut												
Medical												
Gasoline												
Car Tag												
Car Insurance												
Health												
Life Insurance												
Gifts												
Taxes												
Household												
Miscellaneous												
Church												
Allowance												
TOTAL COSTS												
INCOME												
TOTAL INCOME												
DIFFERENCE												
CUMULATIVE DIFFERENCE												

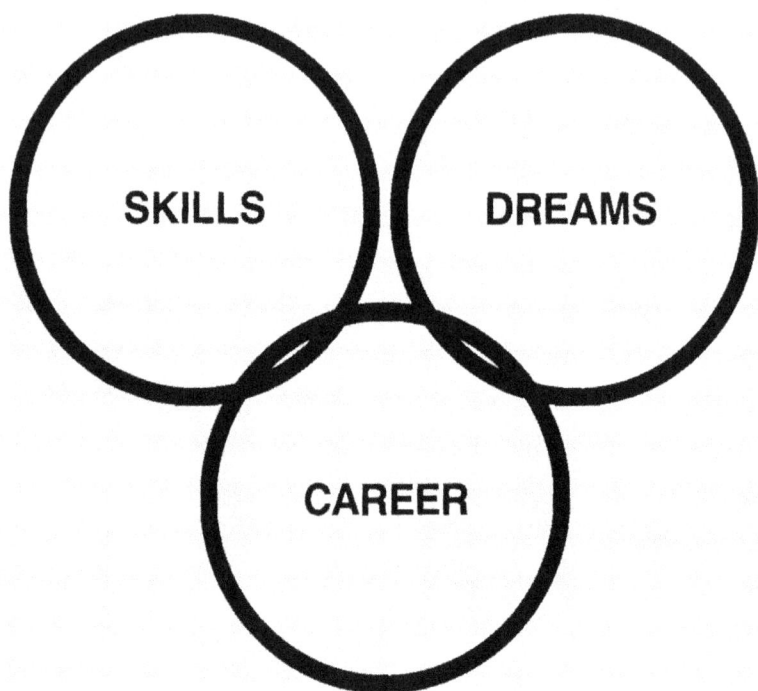

**YOUR CAREER IS WHERE
YOUR SKILLS AND DREAMS
CONNECT**

APPENDIX D

ROADMAP OF OUR LIVES

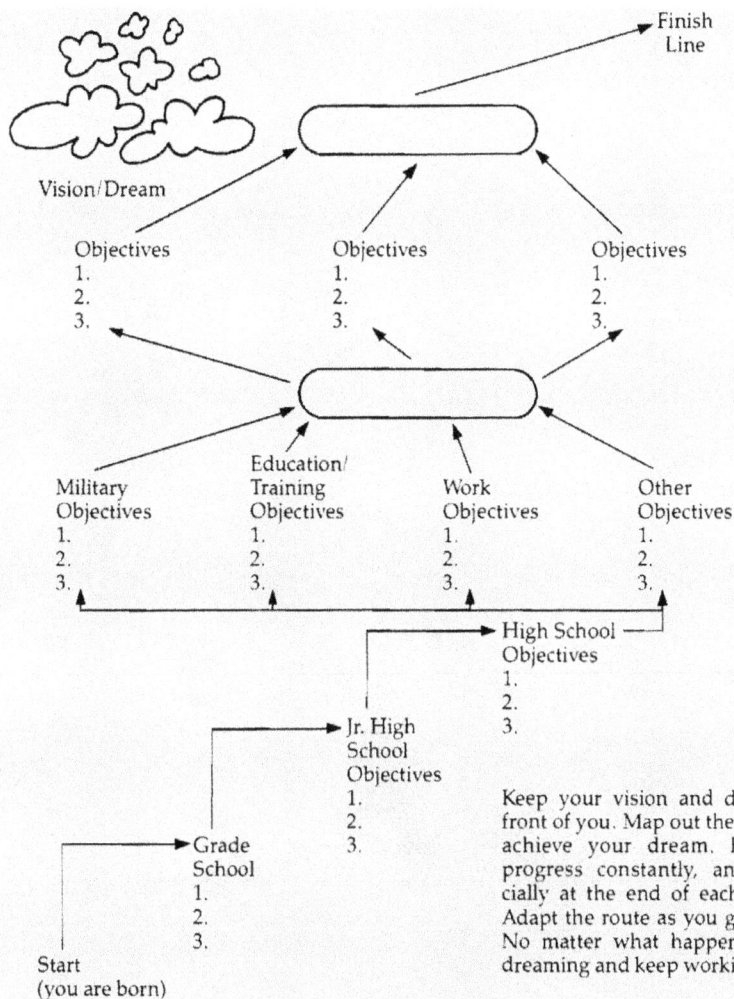

Finish
Line

Vision/Dream

Objectives
1.
2.
3.

Objectives
1.
2.
3.

Objectives
1.
2.
3.

Military
Objectives
1.
2.
3.

Education/
Training
Objectives
1.
2.
3.

Work
Objectives
1.
2.
3.

Other
Objectives
1.
2.
3.

High School
Objectives
1.
2.
3.

Jr. High
School
Objectives
1.
2.
3.

Grade
School
1.
2.
3.

Start
(you are born)

Keep your vision and dream in front of you. Map out the route to achieve your dream. Evaluate progress constantly, and especially at the end of each phase. Adapt the route as you go along. No matter what happens, keep dreaming and keep working.

Appendix E

Common Sense Management: A Biblical Perspective

Management, planning, and organization is not that complicated. It boils down to common sense. According to the Bible, we are to do our work heartily as unto the Lord. Unfortunately, we often neglect this command. The Bible never gives us suggestions. What we are instructed to do are, indeed, commands, and we are commanded to perform the duties of work in such a way that we see God as our boss rather than the person to whom we report. We are to be doers of the Word, and the Word clearly states how we are to conduct ourselves in our work lives. This is revolutionary, even for the twenty-first century. God knows what is best for His people, and His Word states that it is He who promotes. He will allow us to go through seasons during which we might be tested with a trying boss, but we must trust that God knows what is best for us. Perhaps we were to endure such a season to become more patient. Our sanctification process is a lifelong journey and is designed to shift us from relying on our own strength and wisdom to relying on the Holy Spirit. The end result is that we are to be more like Jesus.

Regardless of how one chooses to define "work," we can be certain that schoolwork and volunteer work are included in God's definition. To be sure, work, then, consists of everyday endeavors and may include several types of work for one person. For example, one who works and attends school is meant to perform both tasks with equal vigor and dedication as if purposing to glorify God.

Our efforts would be in vain if they excluded the Lord and His precepts. Work does not have to have a negative connotation. Seldom does a day go by when we don't hear someone complain about having to go to work. God's Word offers many common-sense principles that we can use to our advantage in our work lives as well as in our personal lives. Covey reminds us that we are not human beings on a spiritual journey but rather spiritual beings on a human journey. Once we embrace that common-sense revelation, we should conclude that everything begins and ends with God. One might argue that many atheists have had successful business careers. What is the definition of successful? Anything God permits us to achieve when we exclude Him is achieved only by and through His grace. But the achievement comes without contentment. A widow's mite given from a godly heart brings more contentment than all the riches hoarded. We must remember that God gives us the ability to make wealth. Everything we need to succeed can be found in His Word, through godly counsel and through prayer. If we utilize these, we will soon be astounded at how much common sense we can find in the profound. God may place people in authority over us, or God may give us authority. If we are faithful in the former situation, the latter is sure to come. The secret is to remember that God has authority over all, that His Word is His authority recorded, and that His children have been given authority. How we come to terms with these truths may very well determine how we succeed in this life. We can get caught up in the mysteries of God's Word or we can apply His common-sense principles to manage our lives, our homes, our time, and our work. When we ask Him to teach us to number our days, He will surely direct us to His Word, and because His Word is Truth, even a nonbeliever can benefit from the principles found there. "What a man sows, so shall he reap" is true to both believer and nonbeliever alike. One might ask how the nonbeliever knew to apply a principle he may have never heard of; one answer is common sense.

Here are some common sense principles for better management. Each has a unique title that illustrates the point. Each has a biblical basis.

ICEBERG THEORY: *Stay on the lookout for danger.*

Only by pride cometh contention: but with the well advised is wisdom.   Proverbs 13:10

Without counsel purposes are disappointed: but in the multitude of counselors they are established.
Proverbs 15:22

A wise man sees danger; the fool goes his merry way.
Proverbs 22:3

Hear counsel, and receive instruction, that thou mayest be wise in thy latter end.   Proverbs 19:20

Every purpose is established by counsel . . . .
Proverbs 20:18

For by wise counsel thou shalt make thy war: and in multitude of counselors there is safety.   Proverbs 24:6

PROMOTION THEORY:
Train your replacement; help others develop.

Think about:
> *Moses and Joshua*
> *Elijah and Elisha*
> *Paul and Timothy*
> *Jesus and the 12 Disciples*

MANAGING IS LIKE PARENTING:
Be a responsible manager.

Train up a child in the way he should go (and in keeping with his individual gift or bent), and when he is old he will not depart from it.   Proverbs 22:6

STINGER PRINCIPLE:
Sometimes Christians must tackle problems head on.

Do not hold back discipline from the child, although you

beat him with the rod, he will not die.

You shall beat him with the rod, and deliver his soul from Sheol.   Proverbs 23:13, 14 NAS

Correct your son, and he will give you comfort; he will also delight your soul.   Proverbs 29:17 NAS

CYCLE THEORY: *What goes around comes around.*

Let your eyes look right on (with fixed purpose), and let your gaze be straight before you.

Consider well the path of your feet, and let all your ways be established and ordered aright.
                            Proverbs 4:25-26 AMP

Accordingly then, let us not sleep, as the rest do, but let us keep wide awake (alert, watchful, cautious, and on our guard) and let us be sober (calm, collected, and circumspect).
                            1 Thessalonians 5:6 AMP

But test and prove all things [until you can recognize] what is good; [to that] hold fast.
                            1 Thessalonians 5:21 AMP

Let me warn you therefore, beloved, that knowing these things beforehand, you should be on your guard lest you be carried away by the error of lawless and wicked (persons and) fall from your own (present) firm condition—your own steadfastness (of mind).
                            2 Peter 3:17 AMP

PAY ME NOW, OR PAY ME LATER: *Do it right the first time.*

By wisdom a house is built, and through understanding it is established.   Proverbs 24:3 NIV

A tyrannical ruler lacks judgment.

Proverbs 28:16 NIV

A prudent man sees danger and takes refuge, but the simple keep going and suffer for it.

Proverbs 22:3 NIV

AFRAID TO FAIL: *Like the Nike commercial says, "Go for it."*

When you go to war against your enemies and see horses and chariots and an army greater than yours, do not be afraid of them because the Lord your God, who brought you up out of Egypt, will be with you . . . .

Deuteronomy 20:1 NIV

The steps of a good man are ordered by the Lord: and he delighteth in his way.   Psalm 37:23

DEFENSIVE END THEORY: *Get tough if you have to.*

Finally, my brethren, be strong in the Lord, and in the power of his might.   Ephesians 6:10

If thou faint in the day of adversity, thy strength is small.

Proverbs 24:10

ALAMO THEORY—TOE THE LINE:
Make sure everyone is heading in the right direction.

He who scorns instruction will pay for it, but he who respects a command is rewarded.

Proverbs 13:13 NIV

Then Moses stood in the gate of the camp, and said, Who is on the Lord's side? let him come unto me . . . .

Exodus 32:26

A servant cannot be corrected by mere words; though he understands, he will not respond.

Proverbs 29:19 NIV

He who listens to a life-giving rebuke will be at home among the wise. Proverbs 15:31 NIV

A rebuke impresses a man of discernment more than a hundred lashes a fool. Proverbs 17:10 NIV

LAWN-MOWING THEORY: *There is a way to get organized: Each does what they do best.*

The eye cannot say to the hand, "I don't need you!" And the head cannot say to the feet, "I don't need you!" On the contrary, those parts of the body that seem to be weaker are indispensable.
1 Corinthians 12:21, 22 NIV

Behold, how good and how pleasant it is for brethren to dwell together in unity! Psalm 133:1

VIEW THE WORLD THROUGH (OTHER) COLORED GLASSES: *Respect the view of others.*

And if I have the gift of prophecy, and know all mysteries and all knowledge; and if I have all faith, so as to remove mountains, but do not have love, I am nothing.
1 Corinthians 13:2 NAS

But now God has placed the members, each one of them, in the body, just as He desired.

And if they were all one member, where would the body be?
1 Corinthians 12:18 NAS

STEW IN YOUR OWN JUICE: *Better get your team with you.*

But I did not want to do anything without your consent, so that any favor you do will be spontaneous and not forced.
Philemon 14 NIV

. . . He which soweth sparingly shall reap also sparingly.

2 Corinthians 9:6a

Be not deceived; God is not mocked: for whatsoever a man soweth, that shall he also reap.   Galatians 6:7

SNOWBALL: *Things, events, a course of action can get out of control.*

Now finish the work so that your eager willingness to do it may be matched by your completion of it, according to your means.   2 Corinthians 8:11 NIV

GET YOUR HEAD ABOVE THE CLOUDS: *Take a look where you are going.*

In all thy ways acknowledge him, and he shall direct thy paths.   Proverbs 3:6

A man's heart deviseth his way: but the Lord directeth his steps.   Proverbs 16:9

HOMEOSTASIS: *Be aware that there is an integration-cause-event. We have both: We effect and affect others.*

. . . "If as one people speaking the same language they have begun to do this, then nothing they plan to do will be impossible for them.   Genesis 11:6 NIV

Do not conform any longer to the pattern of this world, but be transformed by the renewing of your mind. Then you will be able to test and approve what God's will is—his good, pleasing and perfect will.

Romans 12:2 NIV

SEED **F**AITH: *Better to give than receive.*

Give, and it shall be given unto you; good measure, pressed down, and shaken together, and running over, shall men give into your bosom. For with the same measure that ye mete withal it shall be measured to you again. Luke 6:38

NATURAL **R**HYTHM: *There is a rhythm to everything.*

Except the Lord build the house, they labour in vain that build it.   Psalm 127:1a

This book of the law shall not depart from your mouth, but you shall meditate on it day and night, so that you may be careful to do according to all that is written in it: for then you will make your way prosperous, and then you will have success.   Joshua 1:8 NAS

To every thing there is a season, and a time to every purpose under the heaven:
A time to be born, and a time to die; a time to plant, and a time to pluck up that which is planted;
A time to kill, and a time to heal; a time to break down, and a time to build up;
A time to weep, and a time to laugh; a time to mourn, and a time to dance;
A time to cast away stones, and a time to gather stones together; a time to embrace, and a time to refrain from embracing;
A time to get, and a time to lose; a time to keep, and a time to cast away;
A time to rend, and a time to sew; a time to keep silence, and a time to speak;

A time to love, and a time to hate; a time of war, and a time of peace. Ecclesiastes 3:1-8

"I'll Be True to You While You're Gone, Honey ... Just Don't Be Gone Too Long": *Don't forget your friends and family.*

Be hospitable to one another without complaint.

As each one has received a special gift, employ it in serving one another, as good stewards of the manifold grace of God. 1 Peter 4:9, 10 NAS

Find Out He is a Christian by How He Acts, Not by What He Says: *Action speaks louder than words.*

Let your light so shine before men, that they may see your good works, and glorify your Father which is in heaven. Matthew 5:16

Yea, a man may say, Thou hast faith, and I have works: shew me thy faith without thy works, and I will shew thee my faith by my works. James 2:18

Having your conversation honest among the Gentiles: that, whereas they speak against you as evildoers, they may by your good works, which they shall behold, glorify God in the day of visitation. 1 Peter 2:12

Be the Best You Can Be: *Don't give the Lord second best.*

And whatever you do in word or deed, do all in the name of the Lord Jesus, giving thanks through Him to God the Father. Colossians 3:17 NAS

Finally then, brethren, we request and exhort you in the Lord Jesus, that, as you received from us instruction as to how you ought to walk and please God (just as you actually do walk), that you may excel still more.
1 Thessalonians 4:1 NAS

NEVER GIVE UP: *Just keep plugging.*

Do you not know that those who run in a race all run, but only one receives the prize? Run in such a way that you may win. 1 Corinthians 9:24 NAS

DO IT WHEN IT IS IMPORTANT: *We tend to put things off.*

Withhold not good from them to whom it is due, when it is in the power of thine hand to do it.
Say not unto thy neighbor, Go, and come again, and tomorrow I will give; when thou hast it by thee.
Proverbs 3:27, 28

SUCCESS—THE WHOLE PERSON: *Success is broader than your career.*

Dear friend, I pray that you may enjoy good health and that all may go well with you, even as your soul is getting along well. 3 John 2 NIV

Do not wear yourself out to get rich; have the wisdom to show restraint. Proverbs 23:4 NIV

BE THERE IN THE MORNING: *Be loyal to the cause.*

Most men will proclaim every one his own goodness: but a faithful man who can find? Proverbs 20:6

Who then is a faithful and wise servant, whom his lord hath made ruler over his household, to give them meat in due season?

Blessed is that servant, whom his lord when he cometh shall find so doing. Matthew 24:45, 46

FAILING TO PREPARE IS LIKE PREPARING TO FAIL

For lack of guidance a nation falls, but many advisers make victory sure. Proverbs 11:14 NIV

THE PRODUCT MUST BE BETTER THAN THE SALES PITCH

Oral Roberts, former President of Oral Roberts University, made this statement at the beginning of a School of Business Marketing Conference at ORU. He was referring to Jesus—and the message to the business audience was that "their product must be better than the sales pitch."

THE O-RING

For lack of guidance a nation falls, but many advisers make victory sure.   Proverbs 11:14 NIV

Plans fail for lack of counsel, but with many advisers they succeed.   Proverbs 15:22 NIV

Listen to advice and accept instruction, and in the end you will be wise.   Proverbs 19:20 NIV

SCRIPTURES RELATING TO PROMOTION THEORY

The Great Commission

And Jesus spake unto them saying, All power is given unto me in heaven and in earth.

Go ye therefore, and teach all nations, baptizing them in the name of the Father, and of the Son, and of the Holy Ghost:

Teaching them to observe all things, whatsoever I have commanded you: and, lo, I am with you alway, even unto the end of the world. Amen.

———————————

Elijah and Elisha

So he (Elijah) departed thence, and found Elisha the son of

Shaphat, who was plowing with twelve yoke of oxen before him, and he with the twelfth: and Elijah passed by him, and cast his mantle upon him.

And he left the oxen, and ran after Elijah, and said, Let me, I pray thee, kiss my father and my mother, and then I will follow thee. And he said unto him, Go back again: for what have I done to thee?

And he returned back from him, and took a yoke of oxen, and slew them, and boiled their flesh with the instruments of the oxen, and gave unto the people, and they did eat. Then he arose, and went after Elijah, and ministered unto him.

1 Kings 19:19-21

. . . Elijah said unto Elisha, Ask what I shall do for thee, before I be taken away form thee. And Elisha said, I pray thee, let a double portion of thy spirit be upon me.

And he said, Thou has asked a hard thing: nevertheless, if thou see me when I am taken from thee, it shall be so unto thee; but if not, it shall not be so.

And it came to pass, as they still went on, and talked, that, behold, there appeared a chariot of fire, and horses of fire, and parted them both asunder; and Elijah went up by a whirlwind into heaven..

And Elisha saw it, and he cried, My father, my father, the chariot of Israel, and the horsemen thereof. And he saw them no more: and he took hold of his own clothes, and rent them in two pieces.

He took up also the mantel of Elijah that fell from him, and went back, and stood by the bank of Jordan;

And he took the mantle of Elijah that fell from him, and smote the waters, and said, Where is the Lord God of Elijah? and when he also had smitten the waters, they parted hither and thither: and Elisha went over.

And when the sons of the prophets which were to view at Jericho saw him, they said, The spirit of Elijah doth rest on Elisha. And they came to meet him, and bowed themselves to the ground before him.

II Kings 2:9-15

The Calling of the First Disciples

And Jesus, walking by the sea of Galilee, saw two brethren, Simon called Peter, and Andrew his brother, casting a net into the sea: for they were fishers.

And he saith unto them, Follow me, and I will make you fishers of men.

And they straightway left their nets, and followed him.

And going on from thence, he saw other two brethren, James the son of Zebedee, and John his brother, in a ship with Zebedee their father, mending their nets; and he called them.

And they immediately left the ship and their father, and followed him.

Matthew 4:19

"*Wisdom* is the principal thing: therefore get wisdom: and with all thy getting get understanding.

Exalt her, and she shall promote thee: she shall bring thee to honor, when thou dost embrace her.

Proverbs 4:7-8

Libraries are full of books on business, planning, management, and other organizational topics, but The Bible remains the best book ever written about how we manage our affairs.

Appendix F

Care and Feeding of a Boss

Care and Feeding of The Boss: *Our attitude toward authority.*

> . . . make my joy complete by being like-minded, having the same love, being one in spirit and purpose. Do nothing out of selfish ambition or vain conceit, but in humility consider others better than yourselves. Each of you should look not only to your own interests, but also to the interests of others.
>
> Philippians 2:2-4 NIV

> How good and pleasant it is when brothers (coworkers) live (and work) together in unity!
>
> Psalm 133:1 NIV

> Anyone, then, who knows the good he ought to do and doesn't do it, sins.
>
> James 4:17 NIV

Care, Feeding of a Boss

Each of us, beginning literally with birth, develops a continuing series of relationships with other people. Without realizing it, we develop relationships with parents, siblings, and other relatives.

As we grow older, we learn to deal with teachers, counselors, scoutmasters, athletic coaches, and pastors.

Later comes college, and some of us even become skilled in the gamesmanship between ourselves and the faculty. Some of us have even had the rare opportunity to get to know a drill sergeant in the military!

Eventually, most of us go to work and begin paying taxes—for which society is grateful. That is when we cease to live off the system and become a contributing part of it. That is when the game of life takes some dramatic changes. At that point, we develop brand new and vital relationships with our new bosses.

A new boss is a person also, one who has gone through the same stages that we have. The difference, and it is a big difference, is that he is one step ahead of us. He has power: the ability to reward and punish, both openly and subtly.

Because of this, we tend to assume that this formidable person has the keen insight to manage us properly. Some of us fail to realize that while we are learning how to deal with him or her, he or she also has a boss to contend with along with all of the problems associated with that relationship.

As I have operated through a wide range of management positions in industry and academia and consulted and advised in a wide range of organizations, I have had the opportunity to study this process, both as player and as an onlooker.

I have noted that the state of uncertainty of all players in the game as to where they stand in the organization is a common denominator that threads through this entire process. This is accompanied by a fair degree of anxiety and apprehension as to what is expected of one by higher management levels and whether one is meeting those expectations.

I believe it is important to recognize this as a natural process and that steps should be taken to cope with it. If these steps relieve the uncertainty, performance might be improved. As starters, I propose the following steps:

1. Ask your boss to develop a list of five key, specific, measurable results he or she wants you to accomplish over the next year.
2. Simultaneously, develop a similar list for yourself—what you believe you should accomplish during the next year.
3. Meet and discuss your lists. Be prepared for some disagreement between them.
4. Reach agreement on what you are going to accomplish. Knowing what is expected of you will give you direction and, thus, increase your sense of security.
5. Now get with it, making sure that you manage your resources well to ensure the results.
6. Keep your boss informed about your progress. He or she does not like surprises.
7. At year end, review the year, see where you stand, and then start the process over again.

What most employees fail to understand is that their primary responsibility is to make sure their boss is successful, to help prevent him or her from making a mistake. You can be sure that your boss wants to be successful. He or she has you on the team to help ensure that success. If he or she has any reason to suspect you of disloyalty or of failure to work for the common good, you are in trouble.

The seven steps listed above help you assure the boss that you are on target with his or her expectations.

It is also important to recognize that *his or her* perception of your contribution is of prime importance and not necessarily your own perception. With this in mind, is it not a good idea to find out from him or her exactly what results is expected?

As you study ways and means to care for and feed your boss, be sure that you honor and respect the responsibility he or she has. Make sure you are loyal to the cause and are making a contribution.

Care and Feeding of an Employee

CARE AND FEEDING OF THE EMPLOYEE:
How we treat those that report to us.

But this I say, He which soweth sparingly shall reap also sparingly; and he which soweth bountifully shall reap also bountifully.

Now he that ministereth seed to the sower both minister bread for your food, and multiply your seed sown.

2 Corinthians 9:6, 10

Employee, Care and Feeding

In the care and feeding of the boss, I pointed out the importance of this relationship, how it should be nurtured, and how to aggressively keep it in good repair and in a healthy state. I suggested that one should develop a set of accountable objectives and results one hoped to achieve during a given time period, discuss these with the boss, and keep him or posted on one's progress. Such a step would provide a firm fix on a goal and on achieving it.

Now we change perspective. We turn our attention the other way and discuss the care and feeding of those who work for us or those under our direction or supervision. What provides the most important job satisfaction to them? What motivates them the most effectively?

In surveys of dozens of large and small businesses, corporations, banks, and nonprofit organizations, I have learned that achievement and recognition are paramount goals of a wide cross-section of people, ranging from welders and bank tellers to upper management. That gives us the first focal point on care and feeding of employees. As one law professor often says in his lectures, "These higher-level needs are as important in our business as blood and air are to the physical body."

Our first step, then, as managers of people is to make sure we recognize these needs and properly feed the souls of those who work for us. Think of all the people who report to you. Ask yourself, When was the last time I provided each of them with some means of positive recognition? This might range from a pat on the back and a warm thank you to a notation on a piece of business correspondence that was well handled or some type of comment in front of a group. If you cannot remember the last time, I suggest that you are derelict and that you should begin to look for some accomplishments to recognize.

After that, you might ask each employee to spell out to you what he or she hopes to accomplish over a certain time frame. Consider your own expectations, and make an agreement. Make sure this is a review process. What better time than this to hand out good, positive reinforcements and to analytically discuss points that have failed to measure up to your expectations?

Caution: You are analyzing performance, not the person. We all tend to safeguard and preserve our self-image; therefore, we respond quickly to an attack on it—real or imagined. If you erred in equating performance with the soul of the person, you have really lost sight of the goal. So, keep your focus on performance.

When reviewing performance, let the employee present his or her evaluation first. He or she will likely be more candid and less defensive if he or she has the first say. This makes your own evaluation easier when your turn comes. You must be genuinely interested and able to project this interest when you talk with your employees. Unless you have their firm support, you are on shaky ground. It is their responsibility to make you successful, and your duty is to help them develop their potentials as individuals.

Be sure you never take credit for others' deeds or ideas. If you take someone's name off a report, for instance, and substitute your own to submit it to your boss, thus receiving the credit, you can be certain the person working for you who really did the work will resent the deceit and will not be disposed kindly toward you in the future. You are that person's only key voice to the next higher level of management. Be sure that you properly represent his or her interests.

Your name is probably well known in each of your employees' homes. Because you are the boss and wield a fair amount of formal and informal power, the employee is ever conscious of your management style. If you doubt this, notice at the next company picnic, banquet, or outing that the employees' families immediately recognize your name.

Many managers are unaware of the important role they play in the psychological well-being of the employee. The employee can shout at his or her spouse, whip the kids, kick the dog, and shake his or her finger at the news commentator or government officials. But he or she is denied using these tactics on you, the boss. He is limited to subtle signals that are sometimes almost unconsciously given. I suggest that you learn to tune in on these signals if you want to know how your people feel. Their proper care and feeding depends on how well you listen and provide nourishment where the hunger is the greatest: self-esteem, achievement, and a feeling of worth.

R. HENRY MIGLIORE, PhD, is a leading strategist for long-term planning for business, sports, and religious leaders. He offers consulting services as well as resources including books, videos, articles, seminars, and training sessions.

He is currently the president of Managing for Success, an international consulting company. Dr. Migliore teaches at the graduate and undergraduate levels at universities worldwide. He was Professor of Management and former Dean of the ORU School of Business from 1975 until 1987. From 1887 to 2003 he was Facet Enterprises Professor of Management at UCT/'NSU Tulsa. From 2003 to date he has worked worldwide as author, visiting professor and consultant. He is currently assisting ORU Global Outreach Center with broadcasts to various target markets worldwide.

He is a former manager of the press manufacturing operations of the Continental Can Company's Stockyard Plant. Prior to that he was responsible for the industrial engineering function at Continental's Indiana plant. In this capacity, Dr. Migliore was responsible for coordinating the long-range planning process. In addition, he has had various consulting experiences with Fred Rudge & Associates in New York and has served large and small businesses, associations, and non-profit organizations in various capacities.

He has made presentations to a wide variety of clubs, groups, and professional associations. Dr. Migliore has been selected to be on the faculty for the International Conferences on Management by Objectives and Strategic Planning Institute Seminar Series and he is a frequent contributor to the Academy of Management. He served for 12 years on the Board of Directors of T.D. Williamson, Inc., and was previously on the Boards of the International MBO Institute and Brush Creek Ranch, American Red Cross/Tulsa Chapter, and is chairman of a scholarship fund for Eastern State College. In 1984, he was elected into the Eastern State College Athletic Hall of Fame. Dr. Migliore has been a guest lecturer on a number of college campuses, including Harvard, Texas A&M, Pepperdine, ITESM, Guadalajara, Autonoma De Guadalajara, and University of Calgary Executive Development programs. He serves on many chamber and civic committees. He was selected Who's Who on a list of 31 top echelon writers and consultants in America.

Dr. Migliore's books have been translated into Russian, Chinese, Korean, Spanish, German, and Japanese.

He has 17 books in total. His next book in process is *Fourth Quarter Redefined*.

HENRY MIGLIORE
4ᵀᴴ QUARTER REDEFINED
THE LEGACY CONTINUES

R. HENRY MIGLIORE, PhD

PRESIDENT OF MANAGING FOR SUCCESS

10839 SOUTH HOUSTON • JENKS, OK 74037 • (918) 299-0007

EMAIL: HMIGLIORE@AOL.COM

WEBSITE: WWW.HMIGLIORE.COM • YOUTUBE: DRMIGLIORE